The Fail-Safe Way On Your Partner and Not Get Caught

A Proven Guide On To Get Away With Cheating In Your Relationship

BY
Henry Ellis Thompson

COPYRIGHT ©

Written By Henry Ellis Thompson

© 2022 CANADA

All rights reserved.

This book is copyright protected. It is only for personal use. You cannot amend, distribute, sell, or paraphrase any part of the content within this book, without the consent of the author or publisher.

The content contained within this book may not be reproduced, duplicated, or transmitted without direct written permission from the author or the publisher.

DISCLAIMER AND LEGAL NOTICE

Please note that the information contained within this book is for educational and entertainment purposes only. All effort has been executed to present accurate, up-to-date, reliable, and complete information. No warranties of any kind are declared or implied. Readers acknowledge that the author is not engaged in the rendering of legal, financial, medical, or professional advice. The content within this book has been derived from various sources. Please consult a licensed professional before attempting any techniques outlined in this book.

By reading this book, the reader agrees that under no circumstances is the author responsible for any direct or indirect losses incurred as a result of the use of the information contained within this book, including, but not limited to, errors, omissions, or inaccuracies.

Under no circumstance will any blame or legal responsibility be held against the publisher, or the author, for any damages, reparations, or monetary loss due to the information contained within this book, either directly, or indirectly.

If trademarks have been used in this publication, they are non-consensual. They lack the consent and sponsorship of the trademark originator.

Any such aspect such as a brand or trademark has been used to bring meaning and illumination to the reader. They however remain the property of the originators and not the creator or publisher of this book.

INTRODUCTION

Don't be such a prude, please. Males just cannot help themselves; they are males. It is not our responsibility to assign blame to others. What we can do is help them make informed decisions and act appropriately. As a result, I wrote this piece, along with a dash of trolling for good measure.

Anyway, I have some friends who, for want of a better term, are experts at juggling women without being caught. As one of them put it, backup. Why not add a personal backup to your software backup? Indeed, I weeded the information out of them because I am a curious person, and I thought this may be a great book, actual war experience from troops with years of experience. They first refused, but when I told them the book would be published with their names if they didn't participate, they quickly provided the advice you are currently reading. Please continue reading.

1st Tip: Have A Lover Who Shares Your Name.

You either choose a woman with the same name as your significant other or compel her to answer to it so you don't get confused when you're angry, passionate, inebriated or all three at the same time. It won't be easy, especially if your wife or girlfriend is named Sammy, but it should work. Discipline is required.

2nd Tip: Look For Younger Mistresses If You Don't Want Children.

Women in their early twenties are frequently less likely to want to commit to children, while also being more vulnerable to the quasi-romantic illusion of having an affair with an older person, or simply someone who is already in a relationship with another woman. They become increasingly demanding and prone to unexpected pregnancies as they age, which you must avoid at all costs until you reach the so-called MILF-divorce phase region, where you will be safe once again. In this circumstance, rubberized things are your greatest friend. Do not believe her when she says she's taking the pill. That is how mistakes are made. You don't want a Glenn Close moment to happen in your kitchen.

P.S. There's also the matter of basic upkeep to think about. Younger women have lesser expectations, and it is well acknowledged that people may rapidly adapt to new, higher standards, but they cannot just return to lower ones. As a result, don't start your romance with a diamond ring, because the next course will be your soul and then some.

3rd Tip: No Home Address, Phone Number, Or Place Of Employment.

Except for nuclear catastrophe, the worst that might happen is your mistress showing up at your house and wanting to meet your other girlfriend.

Women have these hilarious notions, and this is one of them, only you won't be able to laugh very hard, if at all, after drinking Thallium-laced tea. Again, you don't want any dangerous attraction circumstances to occur in your home.

4th Tip: Signed Contracts

This is a bit of difficult advice for those who have a lot of money and/or have minor ties with children. You don't want to lose your Ferrari because you fell in love with a beautiful set of D cups. As a result, you should need your mistresses to sign a contract stating that they will not sue for compensation and that any changes in their status as a result of, as a result of, directly or indirectly caused by their connection with you would not be eligible for claims.

5th Tip : Follow A Rigid Daily Routine.

If you must live recklessly, be certain that your daily schedule is precisely organized. If you've never had late-night meetings before, you can't start now. You can't start missing your wife, family, or anything else all of a sudden. If you can get some adulterations in during working hours, that's perfect. You win twice this way.

6th Tip: Traveling Abroad Is Advantageous.

A short romance while on vacation is an excellent way to avoid any commitment while risking minimal risk.

Always select a mistress from a galaxy far, far away if you must. Keep in mind that males are entirely accountable for the number of children for whom they are liable. Loyalty is proportional to the square root of one's distance from one's spouse or significant other.

7th Tip: Make A Blurry Familial Link.

If you must be seen with your mistress, disguise her as a distant relative from that side of the family to whom no one speaks. You won't come across as a creepy older guy hanging out with a college lady this way. By supporting family members, you may prevent unpleasant questions. That is always valid. However, in this circumstance, you must limit yourself to people of the same race or nationality, since awkward complications may arise.

8th Tip: Do Not Ignore Your Family Obligations Or Overspend.

This is the riskiest thing you could do. Even if you are going on the same trip, you must never use the money you have set up for your children's education to buy your other wife a pearl necklace or to finance a vacation to an exotic island. Not only will you set a dangerous, irrevocable precedent, but you will also increase the entropy of your position. Extracurricular activities need the use of extracurricular funds. It's preferable if she pays.

9th Tip: Don't Brag About It.

One of man's most terrible vices is vanity. Keep all focus on yourself if you chance to be the lady killer who lives the wildlife of a playboy. Many men have made the terrible error of sharing their secrets with acquaintances, so allowing the knowledge to become public. Carry the weight of your pleasure in silence. That is the price tragic heroes must pay for their societal misery.

Here's a little mantra from me. My general recommendation is to avoid being involved with more than one lady at the same time, similar to how anti-virus software should not be used in pairs since it might cause difficulties. In the absence of that, you should be responsible in order to avoid personal humiliation and threats to your family and profession, as well as to guarantee your financial situation is in order.

I also encourage being sensible and choosing the appropriate partners, love, passion, and all that, but if you are average, as most people are, given the divorce rate of roughly 50% globally where applicable, you are extremely likely to make a terrible error. As a result, you are doomed to be miserable. The wisest course of action is to suck it up, but you may bail if necessary. Meanwhile, you compromised little plonker, utilize the aforementioned recommendations as a mitigating middle ground.

Conclusion

The perfect girl possesses intelligence, wit, a respectable and solid education (so she won't need your credit card to seek pleasure), and, preferably, a strong desire not to procreate. It's hard to find, despite the fact that Europe is filled with potential rivals these days, on its way to becoming a modern and defunct Rome. Most men, however, would settle for considerably less, resulting in great pain and disappointment once the wedding is over and the hostage situation involving a couple of kids, or more, arises.

When they're having a good time, some males will wander. Others will do it merely to test if they can get away with it, or for the LULZ. To wit, this fantastic instructional, which is effectively a battle survival manual, was prepared by the world's top fighters, who have a combined infidelity experience of eleven years.

In general, if you feel compelled to cheat despite and because of all of the information presented above, never forget to watch Fatal Attraction beforehand. Should help you sort out your priorities and understand the magnitude of your endeavor's possibilities.

STEP BY STEP GUIDE ON HOW TO CHEAT ON YOUR WIFE

Cheating calls into question your moral standards, whether you're bored, inebriated, or have fallen out of love. Furthermore, if you're in a committed relationship, you should consider why you feel the need to cheat. It's important to remember that cheating isn't easy, and it's not for everyone. So, if you've never cheated and don't want to, congrats, and please get on with your day. If, on the other hand, you're that person - a cheater - well, that explains why you're here.

As a result, I'm here to show you how to cheat on your wife without being discovered or, at the very least, without appearing silly. That is, you should constantly be cautious and avoid potentially dangerous conversations such as whether cheating is wrong or right. Don't do it; instead, let her debate it with her friends.

Again, if cheating would make you feel bad and mess things up, you don't have to do it. But if you're going to do it, there are some ground rules to follow.

The rule "don't drink and drive" is intended to keep you safe on the road. It also applies to cheating. Don't drink while cheating, and if you do, don't become drunk. You don't want to be negligent and injure your sweetheart or anybody else. Let me demonstrate how clever people cheat.

1. Delete All Of Your Phone's Texts.
Putting a password or lock on your phone is not an excuse to conduct irresponsibly. If your wife suspects you of cheating on her, your phone will become the most haunted thing in the home. What if she reads the texts on the phone before it locks? You probably don't want to damage your significant other, so be cautious. Smart folks don't leave any indication of cheating. So, quit being your own worst enemy and erase all those nice text messages. Pretend to be innocent.

2. Put Your Phone Away/Change Your Password
Because she may not suspect anything, not locking your phone can be a really successful tactic. But what if a message comes in while she's holding the phone, or if you forget to erase WhatsApp messages with your side woman and she reads them? Things can get difficult. So, prevent these disaster-in-waiting concoctions by locking your phone. If you feel she has already snooped and knows your existing password, updates it right away. Remember that cheating should be done for pleasure, with no one being harmed, and if it does happen, your wife should not be on the receiving end.

3. Expiration Date For Cheating
If you messed up with your ex, accept the situation as it is. Going to them may stimulate memories that enable the clock to turn back and develop an unpleasant situation, which may not be all that nice. So, for the sake of cheating, avoid becoming connected with people who will ruin the enjoyment. Remember, you're not seeking a long-term relationship, therefore cheat with an expiry date or at the very least know how to cheat with them.

4. Try To Keep Your Falsehood As Basic As Possible.
Even if things grow worse, don't panic if you want to cheat on your wife and get away with it. Compose yourself and come up with a plausible lie. Make it as straightforward as possible. Make a simpler explanation and don't modify it for any reason. Just restrict it to half-lies and half-truths, and you'll be OK. If you're going to freak out and admit everything, don't cheat at all.

5. Establish Your Timetable And Make It Appear Regular.
The greatest approach to get away with your unethical behavior is to keep to a rigid timetable. If your wife detects any abrupt changes in your routine, she may be suspicious and may begin spying on you without your knowledge. Make the situation appear usual by not adding new items.

6. Keep It To A Small Group Or, Better Yet, Just Yourself.

If you're not careful enough to keep your sad renown to yourself, you'll be discovered sooner or later. Keep it to yourself if you want to know how to cheat on your lover and get away with it. If you must tell someone, cut down the list to the most trusted people, and keep in mind that the only person you can totally trust is yourself. You'll be able to cheat peacefully if you use common sense.

7. "Frankly" Talk About It With Your Spouse

If your spouse believes anything is wrong, don't shy away or avoid the subject; otherwise, it may appear that you're hiding something or aren't concerned about their feelings. As a result, pay attention to your partner's concerns and respond properly. Be "honest" in your conversation, apologizing for not understanding they felt the way they did and assuring them that everything is under control. Allow your spouse to communicate their concerns since this can assist you in determining the root of mistrust and resolving it.

8. Modify Your Conduct That Makes Her Suspicious.

If you had an "honest" chat with your spouse, they must have indicated the source of their doubts, which can assist if you adjust the conduct that arouses her suspicion. You can even talk about it and commit to making the necessary adjustments. However, don't somersault your expressions because this will arouse eyebrows. The goal here is to demonstrate some effort in order to maintain confidence, so keep your calm and behave normally.

9. Select One Mode Of Communication.
If you communicate with your secret lover through all of your channels, you're bound to leave some proof behind. With everything going on in life, it might be difficult to keep track of dispersed evidence. So, choosing one channel and sticking to it might help reduce your chances of being detected. One of the safest methods to cheat on your wife and get away with it is to destroy all evidence.

10. Put An End To The Affair
If your spouse still suspects you, even after numerous promises or "altering" your conduct, it is important to quit the affair. Or, at the very least, be patient and wait for everything to return to normal. However, you must be gracious while terminating it, since if the other side is not properly prepared to call it quits, they might cause major problems for you.

SEVERAL METHODS OF CHEATING

There are several methods to harm a spouse, ranging from having a secondary relationship (such as a long-term girlfriend) to having an object affair or having a partner focus on something other than the relationship. However, there are several different ways of cheating. By knowing the many types of infidelity, you can assess whether you or someone you care about is cheating.

1. Cheating Physically
The most visible sort of adultery is physical infidelity or sexual involvement with someone outside your partnership. Though data vary greatly, most suggest that infidelity occurs at a rate of less than 25% of the population.

However, women identify more physical activities as infidelity than men. Women consider emotional interactions with others to be dishonest, although men may not. This implies that how you perceive handholding or a kiss on the cheek may differ depending on your gender, so be explicit with your spouse to avoid future problems.

2. Cheating on the Internet

Online infidelity, sometimes known as cyber adultery, is as damaging to relationships as physical dishonesty. Although males have historically been the more unfaithful sex, women's rates are currently rising due to the emotional nature of online connections.

Online flirtation, photo sharing, or even mutual masturbation through video chat or instant messaging can all be examples of cyber infidelity. Despite the lack of physical contact, these ties may become quite genuine very quickly. Partners who learn their significant other has been cyber cheating are equally devastated, furious, and inclined to end the relationship.

3. Cheating Due to Emotions

Emotional infidelity, defined as having a strong emotional relationship with another person or falling in love with a platonic acquaintance, may be harmful.

However, not all intimate friendships are hazardous, as only a few variables lead to real betrayal. Though some people consider intimate friendships to be emotional infidelity, researchers discovered that ambiguous actions, such as conversing or exchanging personal information, were more closely associated with friendships, and that these people avoided sexual situations.

They did discover, however, that explicit and deceitful approaches, such as lying to one's spouse or participating in flirting behaviors, resulted in greater guilt and more acting on such inclinations toward peers.

If you feel guilty or find yourself thinking sexually about a buddy, you may be engaging in emotional infidelity.

4. Gender Distinctions

Women may be catching up in terms of cheating. Female infidelity may be increasing due to opportunity, affirmation of attractiveness, emotional connection, or the sexual pleasure of a new relationship. Women may also be more vulnerable to online emotional ties that lead to subsequent physical encounters. Men, contrary to popular thought, cheat for emotional connection as well.

They also like to spend months getting to know the lady before plunging into bed. Emotional connection, regardless of gender, is a vital relationship component for avoiding infidelity.

THE MOST COMMON RASONS FOR CHEATING

When you discover your lover has been cheating on you, you may feel upset, furious, and befuddled. But, as bad as it seems when you find out, what you do afterward might be extremely difficult (sorry to break it to you). Moving on, whether alone or with your spouse necessitates a good dose of listening, which is probably the last thing you want to do with someone who has just deceived you. But, believe me when I say that listening to your spouse will help you feel more grounded when things are at their most difficult.

After all, it's either this or letting your mind run wild with solutions to the question "why do people cheat?" that would lead you down an infinite rabbit hole. With all of this knowledge at your disposal, you'll be able to devise a strategy for what happens next, allowing you to emerge on the other side of this.

To be honest, if you ask your spouse why they cheated, you may receive a few versions of "it simply happened," but this is rarely the reality. In truth, there are several reasons why someone would cheat, and it all boils down to the cheater. I've listed out some of the more popular ones for you below.

If one of these reflects what happened in your relationship, consider if it's a deal-breaker for you or whether it's worth seeing a relationship therapist and putting in the effort to rebuild the bond.

First and foremost:

1. They Are No Longer In Love.
Cheating may be a means of undermining a relationship for certain people. "Cheating is merely a means of escaping their marriage." They may want to leave but are too shy to speak up, or they may want to avoid conflict rather than address it.
So, instead of doing something about it, they'll continue to live their comfortable life with you while making new relationships with someone else.

2. Your Partner Felt Abandoned.
"Feeling lonely as a result of your partner's emotional or physical neglect makes the ignored individual more receptive to attention from others or an emotional connection to others." As a result, the neglected individual is more prone to infidelity ".

The early stages of a relationship are frequently fraught with butterflies. However, once the honeymoon period has passed, it can be difficult to retain the thrilling sensation that is generally present at the outset of a new relationship.

Perhaps there aren't as many presents or praises anymore, and some people may feel forced to seek attention elsewhere.

3. They're Acting Out Of Rage Or Vengeance.
When one partner in a relationship cheats, the other may feel compelled to revenge by cheating as well. They believe that this type of retaliation will make the other spouse realize how cruel their actions were. However, this is seldom the case.
"This never ends well since the [relationship] has gotten poisonous to the point where it's best to end." In some cases, a spouse may consider adultery as punishment, even though the other does not. This will inevitably aggravate the relationship.

4. They Have Unsatisfied Wants.
"Everyone has unfulfilled desires." If your spouse, on the other hand, is reluctant to try or compromise, they may find someone who is. Unmet needs in a relationship can range from a lack of sex to a lack of presence.

In my experience, this generally relates to unsatisfied sexual requirements in males, unmet emotional needs in women, or their spouse not showing up for critical occasions.

If moving over infidelity is the aim in this case, then both parties must identify and address these unfulfilled needs. Someone will have to give at some time.

5. They Have A Poor Sense Of Self-Worth.
This motivation for cheating is frequently due to a need for attention.

It generally occurs when one spouse needs more attention than the other can provide, so they seek out someone who will provide it to them—usually repeatedly, making them serial cheaters. In other circumstances, this occurs when a person is continuously put down by their partner, so they walk out and find someone who appreciates them.

6. They Have A Problem With Commitment.

Cheating is a technique for someone who struggles with a commitment to overcome their worries. The commitment-phobic individual who marries anyhow may utilize adultery to deal with their ongoing dread of being imprisoned and to psychologically convince themselves that they aren't actually committed since they may leave at any time. While this is legally correct, they are jeopardizing their connection and, eventually, jeopardizing the ostensibly monogamous relationship they have committed to.

7. They Were Consuming Alcohol.

Though alcohol might cause people to act in ways they would not otherwise, it is not a license to cheat. Alcohol can really motivate you to take action on topics you've been thinking about for a long time. Because alcohol is a dis-inhibitor in general, while someone may slip up and cross a line when drinking, they most likely had the intention to cross the boundary in the first place.

8. They're Bored Or Want To Try Out New Sexual Partners.
If your lover provides you with this as an explanation. Cheating is frequently motivated by anything other than boredom. "It's more a result of not having enough sex or being hesitant to attempt something really significant to their spouse than plain boredom."

If both parties are eager to try to restore the relationship, this is one case when they should both recognize what they may be doing better. Cheating is unforgivable, yet compromise is required to salvage any failed or poisonous relationship.

VARIOUS WAYS CHEATERS ARE CAUGHT

How are cheats apprehended? It's a difficult thing to contemplate, especially if you're in a relationship. You want to be aware of the signals of infidelity, but you also don't want to over think everything and get obsessed with snooping. However, a new poll of 1,000 people on extramarital affairs dating site, discovered a lot about cheating and getting caught.

According to the report, most people are caught cheating during their third affair, and it takes an average of four years for infidelity to be discovered – most usually through text messages.

Only 11% were caught during their first affair, and 12% were caught during their second, which is mind-boggling, especially when you consider that the majority of those caught would say it "never occurred before.

In truth, 86 percent of persons who cheat while married had cheated before they married.
It's difficult to conceal a double existence. It's because that's how we interact these days that stray phone texts and emails are the most common ways cheats get detected. Love letters are a thing of the past!

However, adultery does not always mean the end of a relationship. According to the poll, being caught only results in the termination of a relationship in 15% of situations, therefore 85 percent of couples work through a spouse being unfaithful. Finally, 63 percent of adulterers have been caught at some time, so if you're messing around, odds are it'll come out somehow.

So, how do individuals usually get caught having an affair?
Here's what the survey discovered.

1. Text Messages (39%)
The most prevalent method of detection did not come as a huge surprise – over two-fifths of individuals caught cheating was detected because of their phones.

If you're going to have an affair for an extended period of time, the phone needs to be your difficult spot. Either you're constantly on it or you're constantly hiding it - either way, people are suspicious.

2. E-mails: 22%
Although there was a significant decrease to second place, more than one in every five persons were caught because of their emails. Again, you have all of the same issues as with messages — you check them frequently, hide them, and are shady.

And, of course, it's all too easy to unintentionally leave your email open and have something come up when you least expect it.

3. Being Caught Lying About Your Whereabouts: 20%
Twenty percent of persons were detected lying about their whereabouts. Lying about who you're meeting or where you're going is only effective if everything checks up. If you're doing it on a regular basis, it must be rather simple to slide.

4. Fourteen Percent Of Persons Have Been Picked Out.
Yikes. This one has to hurt, especially if the spotting is done by the spouse. Fourteen percent - an astonishingly high amount – were caught in the act. Not with their trousers around their ankles (though that most likely occurs, albeit infrequently), but when out and about, which still hurts.

5. Obtaining Information From A Friend: 5%
This is either the finest or worst method to find out. 5% of persons learned about their relationship through a friend. On the one hand, it's admirable that those friends had the moral fortitude to do the right thing. On the other hand, the sensation that everyone else knew before you can be quite painful.

There is no foolproof technique to catch your spouse cheating or to discover that someone you care about has been unfaithful, but it's funny that most of the time it comes down to technology.

THE FINEST TIME OF THE YEAR TO CHEAT ON YOUR PARTNER

Is there a better time of year to cheat? Whether you have children or not, there are a few times of year that are unrivaled.

This guide assists in determining the optimum times of year to cheat, based on the activities involved, the likelihood of success, and the available justifications.

1. It's Christmas Week!
Cheating is great during the season of good cheer. For both men and women, the Christmas season provides an opportunity to defraud under the premise of looking for gifts, or the inability to travel due to snow and a crippled transportation system.

Christmas is a terrific time for guys with children to spend hours away from home looking for the ideal gifts for the family. During this week, males might travel to far regions to meet with their partners and do business. If you are thinking of cheating around this time, remember to buy the presents to lessen the risk of suspicion.

Christmas is a perfect time for men and women without children to visit friends' families and do last-minute tasks. These justifications are acceptable and simple to make since they are credible, and they would work well at this time of year. With substantial amounts of snow falling during this time of year, a snow-in might also be a wonderful reason to cheat throughout the Christmas season.

2. The Extended Easter Weekend
Easter is observed towards the beginning of the fall season, no sooner than March 1st and no later than April 22nd. The weekend normally lasts from Thursday night through Tuesday night at midnight. Around this time, most businesses organize workshops and other events.

This weekend is ideal for cheating on your spouse. If you are employed or operate your own business, this may be a terrific moment to cheat. The weekend is also a good time to catch up with pals you haven't seen in a while.

The extended Easter weekend is a perfect opportunity for ladies to indulge. After assisting them for the first two months, women with children would be permitted to leave them in the care of their father under the premise of meeting up with friends, visiting family, or spending time apart from the family. Women without children may be able to use the lengthy Easter weekend as a much-needed getaway to visit relatives or friends.

For guys, the extended Easter weekend is an excellent time to cheat by traveling on corporate trips or meeting up with pals. Traveling to your partner's location may be a great family weekend activity and can help cover up any infidelity. Last-minute business travels are perfect around this time of year for folks who do not have children.

3. Winter Enchantments
Snow and joy bring with them the opportunity to cheat on your spouse. Winter is one of the ideal seasons for cheating. It has plenty of spare time, neatly falling snow, and plenty of excuses to leave the house.

Winter is a better time of year for women with children to cheat than the rest of the year. Because the youngsters are on vacation, they have more leeway in terms of flexibility. They will be distracted by holiday activities and may be left in the care of their siblings if they are not too young.

Winter is a fantastic season for women without children to utilize the family as an excuse to cheat. If you don't have any children, you may deceive yourself by visiting various acquaintances and family members. It would also be reasonable to claim extra work hours.

Men spend more time with their families over the holidays than at any other time of year. It might be tough to avoid spending time with your children or other family members. During this period, it may also be tough to cite employment as an excuse.

Men may take advantage of the expanded number of activities to aid in cheating. You can keep your family busy with events and pleasurable excursions to keep them distracted long enough for you to cheat. If you're lucky, their return trip may be delayed due to inclement weather.

4. Honorable Mention
Most people are turned off by the extreme summer heat, yet it gives an excellent reason to cheat. For men and women with children, you can get away with working evenings during the summer. The graveyard shift will give excellent cover for cheating, and the colder temps will allow you to spend quality time with your lover.

Summer is also ideal for couples who do not have children. You will be able to persuade your spouse of business travels and late hours at work during this season. With such a delightful nocturnal ambiance, it will be a perfect time to cheat in the evenings going late into the night.

Finally, Consider
The optimal time to cheat is determined by the activities you need to engage in with your spouse. It might also be determined by whether you have children and how much effort you put into their daily routines.

Mothers' favorite time of year to cheat is when their children are on vacation. They are free to satisfy their unsatisfied wants without the fuss and bustle of getting them ready for school and creating a comfortable setting in the evenings. For women without children, the optimum time of year to cheat is during the hectic yet beautiful fall season, when their partners are at work.

For guys who do not have children, the optimum time to cheat is over the Christmas season. This winter season surrounding Christmas contains less employment, a hectic holiday schedule for the rest of the family, and a plethora of festivals and events that might be exploited as a diversion to aid cheating. The greatest time of year for men with children to cheat is during the hectic autumn season, when they may cite more work as an excuse to remain out later.

VARIOUS TYPES OF PEOPLE YOU CAN CHEAT WITH

Most marriages are affected by infidelity at some point. While infidelity is as ancient as commitment itself, current technologies and social media have complicated matters by allowing for "micro transgressions" that blur the boundary between emotional and actual betrayal.

However, spouses do cheat, and unfaithful spouses tend to be predictable in their decisions. When a cheating partner decides to cross that boundary, they don't do it with just anybody; it's usually a deliberate move.

In fact, the great majority of extramarital relationships occur between people who already know each other and are in the same social circle.

Cheating men and women generally begin and end their relationships in common places: the office, the gym, a neighbor's house, or online, through an opportunistic encounter or by rekindling a prior romance. What are the similarities between these scenarios?

They all arouse desire and provide opportunity. Although there are few conclusive signals that your spouse is having an affair, once infidelity is discovered, distinct patterns and tendencies emerge. What are they, and what can you do if most cheating spouses fall into the same five scenarios?

1. Ex-Partner
Social networking has not only made it simpler to reconnect with old pals. Facebook, Twitter, and other social media platforms have made it much simpler for husbands and wives to contact ex-significant others.

As much as individuals wish to believe that they may legally be friends with a former lover, marriage and family were claimed to be the outcome of improper boundaries with an ex more frequently than not. This can lead to people attempting to cheat their way out of a failing relationship.

"Contacting one's ex raises the risk of cheating on them when things aren't going well in their present relationship." According to one study, the need to stay around friends may even be an indicator of being a psychopath or narcissist, even when there is no infidelity involved.
Finally, it may be advisable for everyone to avoid the temptation to catch up over a drink.

2. Someone At The Fitness Center

Working out is a terrific way to keep your physical and mental health in check, but it can also be a great opportunity to meet an attractive body with whom to make stupid decisions. Not only is going to the gym one of the most frequent reasons for meeting up with a fling, but nearly three-quarters of cheaters also admitted to working out to make someone other than their spouses happy.

Furthermore, people tend to feel turned on by seeing each other exercise, which may increase the likelihood of finding a sexual partner. While the temptation to cheat may not be the ideal reason to cancel your gym membership and gain weight, it is a terrific motivator to keep focused on your routine and just your workout.

Even better, studies suggest that couples who exercise together stay together. So, if you're concerned about your spouse or simply want to reduce distractions, it could be time to accept their request to join them at yoga.

3. Many Adulterous Temptations Might Be Found Right Across The Street Or Next Door.

According to research, married people commonly talk with their neighbors, owing to the fact that infidelity is typically driven by opportunity.
Surprisingly, facts show that women cheat with neighbors more than men do, owing to men's fear of being caught doing it so close to home.

The majority of males, however, stated that they would not suspect their neighbors of having sex with their spouses. This may assist to understand why some women do it — just because they can.

4. A Colleague At Work
Around 36% of men and women have cheated on coworkers. Mind you, they are only those that acknowledge it. There is also evidence that the better someone is at their work, the more inclined they are to cheat. Many people spend as much time with coworkers as they do with their spouses, and when emotional relationships form from shared challenges, boundaries can rapidly become blurred. It might begin with apparently innocuous jokes about having a "work spouse" or "work wife." "..

"This causes employees to over-identify with one other's difficulties, forcing them to play the loving, supporting role that should be held solely for their spouse," noting that temptation might rise depending on marriage stressors, relationship satisfaction and if their jobs require them to travel frequently with colleagues. "Business trips make it easier and more appealing for people to push those boundaries without arousing the ire of the spouse, who thinks they're working."

5. A Stranger On The Internet
While spouses are more inclined to cheat on someone they know, social media platforms, dating apps, and other websites have made cheating on strangers easier. And they allow you to have an affair even though the majority of us are cooped up at home.

Furthermore, studies show that the Internet may make cheating more than appealing, if not downright addicting, for persons with more impulsive tendencies. "The internet provides a wealth of unlimited options for stranger sex."

SPOTS YOU CAN GO TO CHEAT ON YOUR PARTNER AND NOT GET CAUGHT

Having an affair is exciting, even if there is some risk involved. This appears to mean that while picking a private meeting spot, look for one that is both secretive and enjoyable for both partners. The location should also lower the danger factors.

So, what do you seek when you go out with your secret lover? The solution is straightforward: seek anonymity. When hunting for the appropriate setting, you want to make sure you don't run into anyone you know. The same may be said about your relationship.

There is a lot to consider, which necessitates a lot of planning. As a result, it's a tough business. Cheating partners are always coming up with new ways to meet without being discovered.

Where are individuals meeting for their rendezvous activities?

1. Coffee Houses
It's simple to understand why coffee shops are by far the finest venues to meet up with cheating partners. They are forthright, open, and unconcerned. Nobody can be in the shop at the same time as you and your partner.

2. Accommodations

They provide everything you want for a good dating experience. The eating spaces and restaurants are suitable for first-time meetings. It is best to meet in public places until you are both at ease with each other. It is, in fact, far safer while your affair is still in its early phases.

Hotels are ideal for getting to know each other and deciding how you want things to develop. The majority of hotels have a restaurant and a bar. If you both decide it's time to take things further, you may rent a room at the same facility.

3. Bars And Nightclubs

These are perfect for night-outs, especially if you desire a vivid and dynamic atmosphere to make your night enjoyable. Choose a less noisy bar. It's the greatest place to have a decent dialogue about how to go with your affair.

Meet in a club if you enjoy dancing and loud music. You may rest assured that no one is looking at you. Most bars and clubs are in locations where you can book a room and spend the night if you so desire.

4. Casinos

This is a vibrant spot with hundreds of visitors and out-of-towners. Nobody in this throng will single out you and your date. It offers a peaceful environment for anonymous dating. Have a drink and a round of roulette.

5. On The Side Of The Highway

Cheating partners may decide to leave their cars parked on the side of the road. Partners can get amorous on the roadside between two parked trucks. During a trip, it is fairly unusual to need to pull over. This demonstrates that it is one of the locations where individuals cheat in order to avoid being detected. Just be cautious in each other's vehicles.

6. On A Boat, No Less.

Another great venue to meet your date is for an evening supper on board a boat. You may take your time and enjoy all nature has to offer. The finest part is that no one can stroll in suddenly. In this instance, privacy is assured. Nobody will ever know.

7. At The Movies

After the lights are turned down, the movies may provide a good cover. Partners can meet inside a movie theater. With everyone else concentrating on the action on the screen, you may take a seat in the back. This means that your activities will go unnoticed due to the darkness and loudness in the room.

8. Attend Concerts

This is a fun way to meet your partner. Get those tickets and hop on a train with your significant other to the next musical performance. Nobody will ever consider seeking you there. Enjoy your night out without worrying about glancing over your shoulder. The venue is entirely up to you.

9. Exclusive Evening Dinner

Make your evening more enjoyable by scheduling a catered meal at a location of your choice. Choose a location where you can enjoy your date in solitude. There is no cooking, no fuss, and no dishwashing. Make it a wonderful evening while keeping your privacy in mind.

Find a location that you and your pals don't frequent on a daily basis to keep it discreet. Choose a fantastic location that neither you nor your date is familiar with. This eliminates the possibility of ever being caught.

10. A Picnic

Go to a calm place. Because making supper for two at home may raise suspicions, buy your food and ingredients on the road. Make sure no one follows you on your journey. Remember that the key goal is to remain as unobtrusive as possible.

11. On The Internet

How could we have forgotten about this location? Remember, we're talking about meeting areas where you won't be caught. What could be a more amazing environment than social media? The digitalization of love has occurred. You may meet new individuals online secretly and without breaking a sweat.

You may connect with your spouse and select when and where to meet using a variety of social media channels. Your spouse will never find out what's trending if you hide your tracks effectively.

12. Public Restrooms
Going to the restroom is not a strange thing to do. Washrooms provide an ideal hiding place for unfaithful spouses to carry out their actions. When compared to other community areas, they offer a higher amount of seclusion.

How To Select Safe Meeting Locations

First and foremost, your personal circumstances may provide an easy solution. If you and your date live far apart, a midway point may be the ideal distance from your own area. If it's somewhere you've never heard of before, chances are your husband or wife doesn't go there.

To be safe, try to find a small booth in the back corner when you both arrive. Then have a good time!

Locations Where You Should Avoid Having An Affair

Because of the high hazards of having an affair, it is best to avoid specific settings while meeting with your buddy. You should not meet in either of your houses. Never meet in places where your partners are likely to be. When you play it safe, having an affair may be a lot of fun.

Printed in Great Britain
by Amazon